MW00856991

TEMPTATION

Register This New Book

Benefits of Registering*

- ✓ FREE **replacements** of lost or damaged books
- ✓ FREE **audiobook** – *Pilgrim's Progress*, audiobook edition
- ✓ FREE information about new titles and other **freebies**

TEMPTATION

*Recognizing
and Overcoming
Temptation*

JAMES STALKER

ANEKO
PRESS

We enjoy hearing from our readers. Please contact us at www.anekopress.com/questions-comments with any questions, comments, or suggestions.

Cover Designer: Jonathan Lewis

Editor: Paul Miller

Aneko Press

www.anekopress.com

Aneko Press, Life Sentence Publishing, and our logos are trademarks of

Life Sentence Publishing, Inc.
203 E. Birch Street
P.O. Box 652
Abbotsford, WI 54405

RELIGION / Christian Living / Spiritual Warfare

Paperback ISBN: 978-1-62245-774-8

eBook ISBN: 978-1-62245-775-5

10 9 8 7 6 5 4 3 2

Available where books are sold

CONTENTS

TEMPTATION

There hath no temptation taken you but such as is common to man: but God is faithful, who will not suffer you to be tempted above that ye are able; but will with the temptation also make a way to escape, that ye may be able to bear it.

– 1 Corinthians 10:13

Once when I was going to address a gathering of young men, I asked a friend what I should speak to them about. His answer was, "There is only one subject worth speaking to young men about, and that is temptation."

Of course, he did not mean this literally. He only meant to emphasize the importance of this subject.

Was he not right? Do you remember where the tree that represented temptation stood in the garden of Eden? It stood in the middle of the garden – right at the point where all the walks converged, where Adam and Eve had to pass it every day.

This is a parable of human life. We are out of Paradise now, but the tree of temptation still stands in our life where it stood then – in the middle, where all the roads meet – where we must pass it every day. Every person's success or sorrow depends on the attitude to it that he adopts.

Every person's success or sorrow depends on the attitude to it that he adopts.

There are six attitudes we can have in regard to temptation:

1. We may be tempted.
2. We may have fallen before temptation.
3. We may be tempting others.
4. We may be successfully resisting temptation.
5. We may have outlived, or overcome, certain temptations.
6. We may be assisting others to overcome their temptations.

As I would like these six attitudes to be remembered, let me give them names. I will borrow from the politics of the continent of Europe. Any of you who may glance at times into the politics of France or Germany will be aware that their legislative assemblies are more minutely divided into parties, or groups as they are called, than we are accustomed to.

In American politics there are two main historical parties: Republicans and Democrats. But in Continental parliaments, the members are divided into groups. You read of the group of the Left-Center, the group of the Left, the group of the Extreme Left; the group of the Right-Center, the group of the Right, and the group of the Extreme Right. I do not pretend that even these are all there are, but I will take these as the six names I need for characterizing the six attitudes in which people may stand to temptation.

On the left there are three: first, the group of the Left-Center, by which I mean those who are being tempted; second, the group of the Left, by which are meant those who have fallen before temptation; third, the group of the Extreme Left, or those who are tempters of others.

On the right there are three groups: the fourth group, that of the Right-Center, containing those who are successfully resisting temptation; the fifth, the group of the Right, or those who have endured past their temptations; and the sixth and last, the group of

3

the Extreme Right, or those who are helping others to resist their temptations.

ATTITUDES

<u>Left</u>

1. The group of the Left-Center, or those who are being tempted.
2. The group of the Left, or those who have fallen before temptation.
3. The group of the Extreme Left, or those who are tempters of others.

<u>Right</u>

4. The group of the Right-Center, or those who are successfully resisting temptation.
5. The group of the Right, or those who have outlived their temptations.
6. The group of the Extreme Right, or those who are assisting others to overcome temptation.

Let me briefly discuss these six groups.

1.

THE GROUP OF THE LEFT-CENTER, OR THOSE WHO ARE BEING TEMPTED.

I begin with this one because we have all been in it. We might not have been in the other groups, but we have all been in this one. We have all been tempted. One of the first things we were told when we were quite young was that we would be tempted – that we would have to beware of evil companions. There is not one of us in whose case this prediction has not come true.

Indeed, there is no greater mystery of providence than to understand the unequal proportions in which temptation is distributed. Some people are tempted little in comparison to others, while others are thrown into a fiery furnace of temptation seven times heated (Daniel 3:19).

There are sheltered situations in the world in which a person may be compared to a ship in the harbor, where the waves may sometimes toss a little, but a real storm never comes. There are other people who are like the vessel that has to sail the high seas and face the full force of the tempest. Many of you must know very well what this means. Maybe you know it so well that you feel inclined to say to me, "Preacher, you know nothing about it. If you had to live where we live – if you had to associate with the companions we have to work with and hear the kind of language that we have to listen to every hour of the day – you would know better the truth of what you are saying."

Do not be too sure of that. I might know about it just as well as you do. Perhaps my library is as dangerous a place for me as your workshop is for you. Solitude has its temptations as well as society. Anthony of Egypt, before his conversion, was a carefree and strong young man of Alexandria, but after he was converted, he found the temptations of the city so intolerable that he fled into the Egyptian desert and became a hermit. He later confessed that the temptations of a room in the wilderness were worse than those of the city. It would not be safe to exchange our temptations for those of someone else; everyone has his own.

I believe, further, that everyone has his own tempter or temptress. Everyone on his journey through life meets with someone who deliberately tries to ruin him. Have you met your tempter yet? Perhaps he is sitting by your side at this moment. Maybe it is some-one in whose society you delight to be, and of whose acquaintance you are proud – but the day may come when you will curse the hour in which you ever saw his face. Some of us, looking back, can remember well who our tempter was, and we sometimes still tremble when we remember how close we were to falling over the precipice.

One of the main powers of temptation is the power of surprise. It comes when you are not looking for it. It comes from the person and from the place you least suspect. The day dawns that is to be the decisive one in our life, but it looks like any other day. No bell rings in the sky to warn us that the hour of destiny has come, but the good angel that watches over us is waiting and trembling. The fiery moment arrives. Do we stand or do we fall? If we fall, that good angel goes flying away to heaven, crying, "Fallen, fallen, fallen!"

2.

THE GROUP OF THE LEFT, OR THOSE WHO
HAVE FALLEN BEFORE TEMPTATION.

Although I do not know all of you, I know human nature well enough to be certain that there are some reading this or hearing this who are whispering sadly in their hearts, "This is the group I belong to. I have fallen before temptation. It may not be known, and it may not even be suspected, but it is true."

To these people, I bring a message of hope today.

Satan, the great tempter, has two lies with which he pursues us at two different stages. Before we have fallen, he tells us that one fall does not matter. He says that it is just a little matter and we can easily recover ourselves again. Then, after we have fallen, he tells us that it is hopeless, that we are given over to sin and do not need to attempt to rise.

Both are false.

It is a terrible falsehood to say that to fall once does not matter. Even by one fall there is something lost that can never be recovered again. It is like when an infinitely precious vessel is broken. It can be put back together, but it will never be again as if it had not been broken. And besides, one fall leads to others. It is like trying to walk up a hill upon very slippery ice. In attempting to rise, you are carried away again farther than ever.

Moreover, we give others a hold over us. If we have sinned with others, to have sinned even once involves an indirect pledge that we will sin again, and it is often almost impossible to get out of such a false position. May God keep us from believing the devil's lie that to fall once does not matter.

But then, if we have fallen, Satan works on us with the other lie – that it is of no use to attempt to rise because you cannot overcome your besetting sin. This is even more false. To those who feel themselves fallen, I come in Christ's name to say, "Yes, you may rise. If we could ascend to heaven today and scan the ranks of the blessed, we would find multitudes among them who were once sunk as low as man can fall. But they are washed, they are sanctified, they are justified in the name of our Lord Jesus and by the Spirit of our God (1 Corinthians 6:11). And so may you be.

It is, I know, a doctrine that may be abused, but I will not hesitate to preach it to those who are fallen and are yearning for deliverance. Augustine says that out of our dead sins we may make stepping-stones to rise to the heights of perfection. What did he mean by that? He meant that the memory of our falls may create in us such a humility, such a distrust of self, such a constant clinging to Christ that we never could have had if we had not fallen.

> The memory of our falls may create in us such a humility, such a constant clinging to Christ that we never could have had if we had not fallen.

Does not the Scripture itself go even further? David fell as deep as man can fall, but what does he say in that great fifty-first Psalm (v. 13), in which he confesses his sin? Anticipating forgiveness, he says, *Then will I teach transgressors thy ways; and sinners shall be converted unto thee.*

And what did our Lord Himself say to Peter about his fall? *When thou art converted, strengthen thy brethren* (Luke 22:32). A person may derive strength to give to others from having fallen. He may have sympathy toward those who have stumbled. He may be able to describe the steps by which to rise, as no one else can. Thus, by God's marvelous grace, out of the eater may come forth meat, and out of the strong may come forth sweetness (Judges 14:14).

3.

THE GROUP OF THE EXTREME LEFT, OR THOSE WHO ARE TEMPTERS OF OTHERS.

These three groups on the left form three stages of a natural descent:

First, tempted.

Secondly, fallen.

Then, if we have fallen, we tempt others to fall.

This is quite natural. If we are down ourselves, we try to get others down beside us. There is a satisfaction in it. To a soul that has become stained, a soul that is still white is an offense. It is said of some, "They do not rest unless they have done wrong, and they are unable to sleep unless they have caused someone to fall."

I do not think there is anything else in human nature as diabolical as the delight that the wicked feel in making others like themselves. Have you never seen it? Have you never seen a group of evildoers deliberately attempt to ruin a newcomer, mocking his innocence and enticing him to their sinful activities? Then, after they succeeded, they rejoiced over his fall as if they had won a great triumph. Human nature can sink so low.

Sometimes it may be self-interest that makes a person a tempter. The sin of another may be necessary to secure some end of his own. The dishonest merchant, for his own gain, undermines the honesty of his apprentice. The employer, in a hurry to be rich, tempts his employees to break the Sabbath. The tyrannical landlord forces his tenants to vote against their consciences. There are entire trades that flourish on other people's sins.

The most common way, though, to become a tempter is through thoughtlessness. I contend that we have no compassion for each other's souls. We trample about among these most brittle and infinitely precious things as if they were common goods, and we tempt one another and ruin one another without even being aware of it. It might be true indeed that no one who goes to the place of woe goes there alone; possibly everyone takes at least one person with him.

> No one who goes to the place of woe goes there alone; possibly everyone takes at least one person with him.

I hear it said nowadays that the fear of hell no longer moves people's minds, and that preachers should no longer make use of it as a motive in religion. Well, I confess that I fear it myself; it is still a motive to me.

However, I will tell you what I fear ten times more. What! Is there anything that someone can fear ten times more than the fire that will never be quenched (Mark 9:48)? Yes! It is to meet someone there who will say, "You have brought me here. You were my tempter. If it were not for you, I might never have come to this place of torment." God forbid that this would ever be said to me by anyone. Will it be said to any of you?

Let us turn away from this side of our subject and look at the bright side – at the three groups on the Right.

4.

THE GROUP OF THE RIGHT-CENTER, OR THOSE WHO ARE SUCCESSFULLY RESISTING TEMPTATION.

Not very long ago, I happened to come across a letter that was written by a young man attending one of the great English universities. One day, two or three fellow students entered his room and asked him to join them in some amusement of a questionable kind that they were considering. On the spur of the moment, he promised to join them, but after they had gone, he began to wonder what his parents would say if they knew. His home was a godly and a very happy one, and the children's close ties to their parents prevented them from keeping any secrets from them. He thought of his home, and he began to wonder whether what he had promised to do might not cause pain there. He was afraid it would, and so he quickly and honestly went and told his companions that his arrangement with them was off until he was able to ask his parents about it. The letter I saw was the inquiry. It affected me deeply to read it, for it was easy to understand how much manliness was required to do that which might be interpreted as unmanly.

The memory of that man's home came to him in the hour of temptation and made him strong to resist. I marvel that this influence does not prove to be a rescuing power more often than it does. Young men and women, when you are tempted, think of home. I have been a minister in a rural town, and I think that if you could realize the effect produced by the news coming from the city of a son fallen and disgraced – if you could realize the mother's dismay, the father's wounded reaction, and the silent, tearful circle as I have seen them – it would make you fling the cup of temptation from your lips, no matter how persuasive the hand was that offered it.

However, this will not always be a strong enough motive in the struggle with temptation. There will come times when you are tempted to a strong sin that will seem to you absolutely safe from discovery and not likely to inflict the slightest harm on your circumstances. In such situations, nothing will sustain you if you do not respect your own nature and stand in awe of your own conscience. No, even this is not enough. The only effective defense is that which Joseph used when he was severely tempted in this very way: *How then can I do this great wickedness, and sin against God?* (Genesis 39:9).

There are secret battles fought and victories won on this ground that are never heard of on earth, but are essentially more glorious than many victories that are trumpeted far and wide by the breath of fame. There is more of courage and manhood needed for these battles and victories than for walking up to the cannon's mouth. Walking up to the cannon's mouth! Many soldiers could do that who could not say "No" to two or three companions pressuring him to enter the tavern.

> There is more of courage needed for these secret battles and victories than for walking up to the cannon's mouth.

Not long ago, I was speaking to a soldier who told me that many times in the barracks he was the only man to go down on his knees and pray out of twenty or thirty men, and he did it among barrages of curses and ridicule. Do you think walking up to the cannon's mouth would have been difficult to that man? Such victories have no record on earth, but you can be sure that they are widely heard of in heaven, and there is One there who will not forget them.

5.

THE GROUP OF THE RIGHT, OR THOSE WHO HAVE OUTLIVED THEIR TEMPTATIONS.

I do not intend to dwell long on this point, but I would like to at least mention it, for there is great encouragement contained in it for some who may be enduring the very hottest fires of temptation. Maybe your situation is so unbearable that you often say, "I cannot stand this much longer; if it continues as it is, I will break. One day I will fall into the hands of Saul" (1 Samuel 27:1).

No, you will not. I call upon you to take courage. As one encouragement, I say that you will yet outlive your temptation.

That which is a temptation at one period of life may not be a temptation at all at another. To a child there may be an irresistible temptation in a sweet dessert that an adult would not take much interest in. Some of the temptations that are now the most painful to you will in time be completely outlived. By some turn of providence, God may lift you out of the position where your temptation lies, or the person from whom you mainly suffer may be removed from your neighborhood. The unholy fire of passion, which now you must struggle to keep out of your heart, may, through the mercy of God who sets men in families, be burned away and replaced by the holy fire of love burning on the altar of a virtuous home.

> **Even the ungodly are forced at last to honor a consistent Christian life.**

The laughter and ridicule that you may now be enduring for your Christian profession will, if you only have patience, be changed into respect and veneration – for even the ungodly are forced at last to honor a consistent Christian life.

In these and other ways, if you only have patience, you will outlive temptation – although I do not suppose we will ever be entirely out of its reach in this world. I do not believe that we will ever be beyond the need of these two admonitions: *Watch and pray, that ye enter not into temptation* (Matthew 26:41), and *Let him that thinketh he standeth take heed lest he fall* (1 Corinthians 10:12).

6.

THE GROUP OF THE EXTREME RIGHT, OR THOSE WHO ARE ASSISTING OTHERS TO OVERCOME TEMPTATION.

On the Right there is an upward progress, just as on the Left there was a downward one. The first step is to be successfully resisting temptation; a higher step is to have outlived, or overcome, temptation; the highest step of all is to help others to resist it. Although I do not say that this must be the chronological order, it is the order of honor.

This group of the Extreme Right is the exact opposite of the group of the Extreme Left. Those in the latter group are tempting others to fall, while those in this group are encouraging and helping others to stand firm. No one should be satisfied until he is in this noble group.

There are many ways in which we may assist others with their temptations. A bighearted man will often do so without being aware of it. His very presence, his appealing masculinity, and his massive character act as an encouragement to younger men and help them remain steadfast. I do not know anything as much to be coveted in old age as to have someone say to you, "Your example, your presence, and your encouragement were like a protecting arm put around my stumbling youth and helped me over the perilous years." My brothers and sisters, if a few people can honestly say this to us in the future, will it not be better than Greek and Roman fame?

Many are helping the young against their temptations by providing them with means of spending their free time innocently and profitably. Our leisure time is the problem. While we are at work, there is not as much temptation to fear, but it is in the hours of leisure – the hours between work and sleep – that temptation finds us, and that is when we are lost. Therefore I say that there is no more Christian work than to provide people with opportunities of spending time profitably.

Christ is the most effective defense, and nothing else can really be depended on.

But by far, the best way to help people with their temptations is to bring them to Christ. It may be of some service to someone if, in the time of temptation, I put the sympathetic arm of a brother around him, but it is infinitely better if I can get him to allow Christ to put

His strong arm around him. This is the most effective defense, and nothing else can really be depended on.

I think I have been speaking to your hearts and to your experience. This is not a subject that is debatable; it is our very life. Let me say a final word about how to deal with temptation.

How are you dealing with your own? There are two ways, which may be called the Method of Resistance and the Method of Counter-Attraction. I have seen them illustrated by two legends of ancient Greek mythology, and with these I will close.

The one legend is that of Ulysses, the great traveler of those mythical times. It is said that once in his wanderings, he came to the spot on the southern shore of Italy where the Sirens lived. The Sirens were a type of mermaid. They were beautiful in person and especially in voice, but destructive in soul. They used to sing on the shore as ships were passing by, and with their sweet songs allure the mariners to their destruction upon the rocks. But Ulysses was a wise and clever traveler, and as he was aware of the danger, he took measures to provide for his safety.

He assembled the sailors, explained the situation, and told them they must row past the fatal spot for their lives. Then he stuffed their ears with wax so that they could not hear a sound. His own ears were not stuffed, but he made the sailors bind him hand and foot to the mast. In this condition they reached the place that had been fatal to so many. The Sirens saw them and came out and sang their sweetest. The sailors, hearing nothing because of the wax in their ears, rowed stubbornly on. Ulysses heard the singing, and was so enraptured that he would have done anything to reach the shore, but since he was bound hand and foot, he could do nothing to influence the direction of the ship. They rounded a cape and the danger was past.

The other story is about the Argonauts, who were sailing to Pontus in search of the Golden Fleece. They also had to pass the same dangerous place. However, in their ship they had Orpheus, the great poet and singer of those mythical times, with them in their ship. It was said that he sang so ravishingly that lions and tigers came crouching to his feet, and even rocks and trees followed where he went. Every day he poured his enchanting strains into the ears of the Argonauts.

Eventually they arrived at the dangerous spot, and the Sirens, seeing them, came forth and sang their sweetest. But the Argonauts only laughed at them and passed on. How were they able to do so? It was because the charm of the inferior music had been broken by that which was superior.

These two stories illustrate the two ways of meeting temptation. The one is the method of restraint, when we keep ourselves from sin by sheer strength or force, as Ulysses saved himself from the allurement that was drawing him. Of course, this is far better than yielding to temptation.

The other method is the secret of Christianity. The attraction of temptation is overcome by a counter attraction. The love of Christ in the heart destroys the love of sin, and the new song of salvation enables us to despise the siren song of temptation and pass it by. That person who sails the seas of life is only really safe when he carries on board the Divine Orpheus, whose heavenly music is daily sounding in his soul.

JAMES STALKER – A BRIEF BIOGRAPHY

James Stalker was born in Crieff, Scotland, on February 21, 1848. He was educated at the University of Edinburgh, and he was ordained as a minister of the Free Church of Scotland in 1874. He began his ministry at St. Brycedale, in Kirkcaldy, in that same year, and in 1887 he began pastoral duties at St. Matthew's in Glasgow. He was also a professor of church history at the Free Church College in Glasgow. James Stalker was a widely known preacher of his day in Scotland and America. He also authored many books, the two best known of which are his *Life of Jesus Christ* and his *Life of St. Paul*.

He was known for speaking out from the pulpit against the social sins of his day. He supported the movement for revival and supported the meetings of D. L. Moody and Ira Sankey when they came to Scotland in 1873. Rev. Stalker often visited America, where he preached at many colleges and seminaries, including at Yale in 1891. He gave some advice to the students at Yale about preaching. He said:

It is true of every appearance that a minister makes before a congregation. Unless he has spent the week with God and received Divine communication, it would be better not to enter the pulpit or open his mouth on Sunday at all. There ought to be on the spirit, and even on the face of a minister, as he comes forth before men, a ray of the glory that was seen on the face of Moses when he came down among the people with God's message from the mount.

James Stalker encouraged ministers to spend much time in communion with God. "The soul must be in touch with God and enjoy golden hours of fresh revelation." He explained the most common cause of failure in pastoral ministry:

Either we have never had a spiritual experience deep and thorough enough to lay bare to us the mysteries of the soul; our experience is too old, and we have repeated it so often that it has become stale to us; we have made reading a substitute for thinking; we have allowed the number and the pressure of the duties of our office to curtail our prayers and shut us out of our studies; or we have learned the professional tone in which things ought to be said, and we can fall into it without present feeling. Power for work like ours is to be acquired in secret; it is only the man who has a large, varied, and original life with God who can go on speaking about the things of God with fresh interest; but a thousand things happen to interfere with such a prayerful and meditative life. . . . The hearers may not know why their minister, with all his gifts, does not make a religious impression on them; but it is because he is not himself a spiritual power.

James Stalker preached and wrote with power, for He communed with God, faithfully followed Jesus, walked in the Spirit, and boldly proclaimed the gospel. James Stalker died on February 5, 1927.